The
★ ★
UNITED
STATES

PRESIDENTS

James A. GARFIELD

Megan M. Gunderson

Big Buddy Books

An Imprint of Abdo Publishing
abdopublishing.com

abdopublishing.com

Published by Abdo Publishing, a division of ABDO, PO Box 398166, Minneapolis, Minnesota 55439.
Copyright © 2017 by Abdo Consulting Group, Inc. International copyrights reserved in all countries. No part of this book may be reproduced in any form without written permission from the publisher. Big Buddy Books™ is a trademark and logo of Abdo Publishing.

Printed in the United States of America, North Mankato, Minnesota
062016
092016

THIS BOOK CONTAINS
RECYCLED MATERIALS

Design: Sarah DeYoung, Mighty Media, Inc.
Production: Mighty Media, Inc.
Editor: Lauren Kukla
Cover Photograph: Getty Images
Interior Photographs: Alamy (pp. 9, 13); Corbis (pp. 5, 7, 29); Library of Congress (pp. 6, 7, 15, 17, 21, 23, 27); Ohio Historical Society (p. 11); Picture History (pp. 19, 25)

Cataloging-in-Publication Data

Names: Gunderson, Megan M., author.
Title: James A. Garfield / by Megan M. Gunderson.
Description: Minneapolis, MN : Abdo Publishing, [2017] | Series: United States
    presidents | Includes bibliographical references and index.
Identifiers: LCCN 2015045622 | ISBN 9781680780949 (lib. bdg.) |
    ISBN 9781680775143 (ebook)
Subjects: LCSH: Garfield, James A. (James Abram), 1831-1881--Juvenile
    literature. 2. Presidents--United States--Biography--Juvenile literature. |
    United States-- Politics and Government--1881-1881--Juvenile literature. Classification: DDC
973.8/4092092 [B]--dc23
LC record available at http://lccn.loc.gov/2015045622

Contents

James A. Garfield

James A. Garfield served as the twentieth president of the United States. As president, he fought for **civil service reform**. Sadly, his term lasted just six months.

In 1880, Garfield was elected to the US Senate. But he was elected president before he could take his seat. Garfield took office in 1881.

That summer, President Garfield was shot by an **assassin**. Eighty days later, he died. He had given most of his life to public service.

Timeline

1831

On November 19, James Abram Garfield was born in Orange Township, Ohio.

1859

Garfield was elected to the Ohio state senate.

1858

Garfield married Lucretia Rudolph.

1860

Garfield worked on **Republican** Abraham Lincoln's presidential campaign.

1880
In November, Garfield won the presidential election.

1861
Garfield became a **lawyer**. He began fighting in the **American Civil War**.

1881
Charles Guiteau shot Garfield on July 2. On September 19, James A. Garfield died.

Growing Up in Ohio

James Abram Garfield was born in Orange Township, Ohio, on November 19, 1831. His parents were Abram and Eliza Garfield.

Before James was two years old, his father died. In 1848, James left home to work. But his mother urged him to go to school.

★ FAST FACTS ★

Born: November 19, 1831

Wife: Lucretia Rudolph (1832–1918)

Children: seven

Political Party: Republican

Age at Inauguration: 49

Year Served: 1881

Vice President: Chester Arthur

Died: September 19, 1881, age 49

James got a job leading the mules that pulled a canal boat.

Eager Student

In 1849, James entered Geauga Academy in Chester, Ohio. It was just 12 miles (19 km) from his home. To help James get started in school, his mother gave him $17. It was her life's savings.

However, James still needed to earn extra money. So during his first year, he did odd jobs. The next winter, he taught school in Chagrin Falls, Ohio.

★ **DID YOU KNOW?** ★

Eliza Garfield was the first president's mother to attend her son's inauguration.

At Geauga, James was an excellent student. He studied grammar, mathematics, and philosophy.

In 1851, James entered Western Reserve Eclectic Institute in Hiram, Ohio. Today, this school is called Hiram College. There, James was a good student. He also became known as a strong public speaker.

During his second year at the school, James began teaching. He saved money so he could continue his education on the East Coast. In September 1854, James moved to Williamstown, Massachusetts. There, he entered Williams College. In August 1856, James spoke at his **graduation**.

At Williams College, James was a good student. He was also the leader of several societies, including a literary club.

Political Teacher

After **graduation**, Garfield returned to the Eclectic Institute as a teacher. In 1857, he became president of the school. Then, in 1858, Garfield married Lucretia Rudolph.

Meanwhile, Garfield had become interested in **politics**. He soon **supported** the **Republicans**. Like Garfield, Republicans were against slavery.

Garfield was elected to the Ohio state senate in 1859. In 1860, he worked for Abraham Lincoln's presidential campaign. During this time, Garfield was also studying law.

The Garfields had five surviving children. One son and one daughter died when they were babies.

Civil War Officer

In 1861, Garfield passed the test to become a **lawyer**. However, the **American Civil War** also began that year. Garfield joined the army.

On January 10, 1862, Garfield led troops to win the Battle of Middle Creek in Kentucky. The following month, he fought in the Battle of Shiloh in Tennessee.

In November, Garfield was elected to the US House of **Representatives**. However, he would not take office until December of the next year.

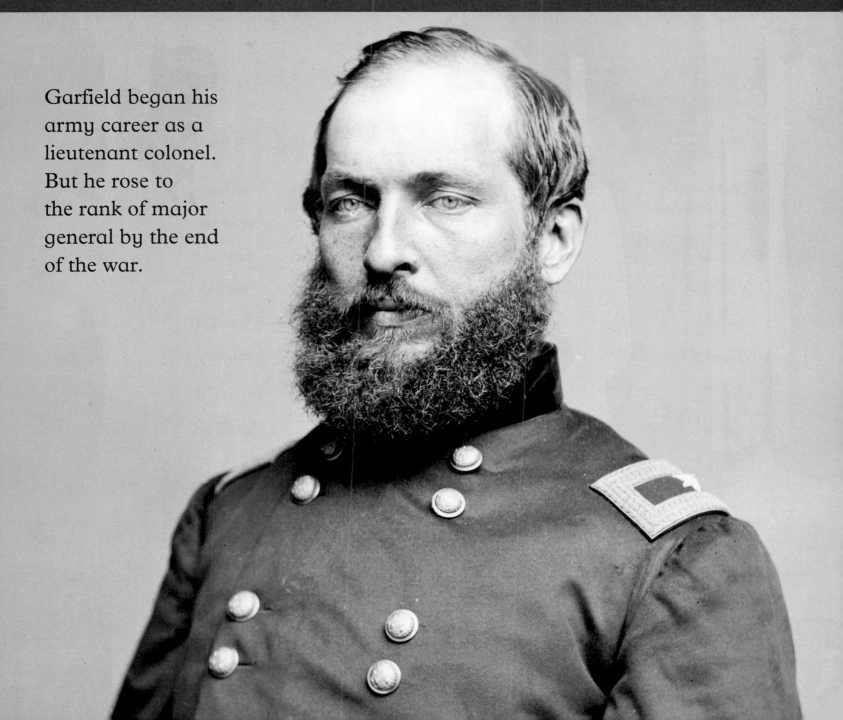

Garfield began his army career as a lieutenant colonel. But he rose to the rank of major general by the end of the war.

Off to Washington

In 1863, the **American Civil War** continued. Abraham Lincoln was now president. He hoped Garfield would take his seat in the House. So, Garfield left the army. In December 1863, he went to Washington, DC.

In Congress, Garfield fought against substitution. This practice allowed men to get out of military service. They hired men to take their places instead of serving themselves. Garfield also fought for equal pay for African-American soldiers.

In Congress, Garfield (*center*) served as chairman of the Committee on Military Affairs. In this position, he used his experience to help run the Union army.

After the war, Congressman Garfield sided with the Radical **Republicans**. They felt the Southern states should guarantee African Americans equal rights. So, Garfield favored a strong **Reconstruction** policy for the South.

Education remained important to Garfield. So, he became a leader in setting up the US Department of Education. Then, early in 1880, Garfield was elected to the US Senate. But he never joined the Senate. Before he could, Garfield was **nominated** for president.

★ DID YOU KNOW? ★

President James A. Garfield had the second-shortest term as president in US history.

Congressman Garfield helped create the US Geological Survey. This government agency studies public lands and offshore areas.

Surprise Nominee

In 1880, the **Republicans** held a meeting to talk about the next election. There, Garfield **supported** John Sherman for president. Others also wished to be **nominated** for president.

Garfield gave a speech nominating Sherman. But in the middle of it someone yelled, "We want Garfield!" Soon, the **delegates** began voting. But after 33 votes, no one had won.

Then, 16 Wisconsin delegates voted for Garfield. He began receiving more votes. In the end, he was chosen to run for president.

Chester Arthur was chosen to run as Garfield's vice president. He became president upon Garfield's death.

President Garfield

In November 1880, Garfield was elected president. It was one of the closest elections on record. He was sworn in on March 4, 1881.

President Garfield promised **civil service reform**. In the past, **politicians** had **rewarded** their **supporters** with civil service jobs. Garfield believed the best person should get the job. His decisions upset people who were hoping to get civil service jobs.

★ SUPREME COURT APPOINTMENT ★

Stanley Matthews: 1881

Garfield beat his opponent, General Winfield Scott Hancock, by fewer than 10,000 votes.

During his presidency, Garfield also faced problems with the US Post Office. Contracts were given to private individuals for certain delivery routes. However, some individuals were charging more money than their contracts said they could.

This became known as the Star Route **Scandal**. Garfield **appointed** Thomas L. James to **investigate** the problem. James soon proved widespread wrongdoing. The men involved went to **trial** after Garfield's term in office.

★ DID YOU KNOW? ★

James Garfield could write with both his left hand and his right hand at the same time.

PRESIDENT GARFIELD'S CABINET

March 4, 1881–September 19, 1881

★ **STATE:** James G. Blaine
★ **TREASURY:** William Windom
★ **WAR:** Robert Todd Lincoln
★ **ATTORNEY GENERAL:** Wayne MacVeagh
★ **NAVY:** William Henry Hunt
★ **INTERIOR:** Samuel Jordan Kirkwood

Assassination

In summer 1881, Garfield planned to visit Mrs. Garfield, who was in New Jersey. On July 2, Garfield waited for a train at the railroad station. There, a man shot him.

The man was Charles Guiteau. He was angry because Garfield had refused to give him a job. On September 19, Garfield died of his wounds.

James A. Garfield served his country for most of his life. He believed in hard work and the value of education. His **assassination** helped lead to **civil service reform**.

Guiteau fired two shots. One hit Garfield in the back, and the other grazed his arm.

Office of the President

Branches of Government

The US government has three branches. They are the executive, legislative, and judicial branches. Each branch has some power over the others. This is called a system of checks and balances.

★ Executive Branch

The executive branch enforces laws. It is made up of the president, the vice president, and the president's cabinet. The president represents the United States around the world. He or she also signs bills into law and leads the military.

★ Legislative Branch

The legislative branch makes laws, maintains the military, and regulates trade. It also has the power to declare war. This branch includes the Senate and the House of Representatives. Together, these two houses form Congress.

★ Judicial Branch

The judicial branch interprets laws. It is made up of district courts, courts of appeals, and the Supreme Court. District courts try cases. Sometimes people disagree with a trial's outcome. Then he or she may appeal. If a court of appeals supports the ruling, a person may appeal to the Supreme Court.

Qualifications for Office

To be president, a candidate must be at least 35 years old. The person must be a natural-born US citizen. He or she must also have lived in the United States for at least 14 years.

Electoral College

The US presidential election is an indirect election. Voters from each state choose electors. These electors represent their state in the Electoral College. Each elector has one electoral vote. Electors cast their vote for the candidate with the highest number of votes from people in their state. A candidate must receive the majority of Electoral College votes to win.

Term of Office

Each president may be elected to two four-year terms. The presidential election is held on the Tuesday after the first Monday in November. The president is sworn in on January 20 of the following year. At that time, he or she takes the oath of office.
It states:

I do solemnly swear (or affirm) that I will faithfully execute the office of President of the United States, and will to the best of my ability, preserve, protect and defend the Constitution of the United States.

31

Line of Succession

The Presidential Succession Act of 1947 states who becomes president if the president cannot serve. The vice president is first in the line. Next are the Speaker of the House and the President Pro Tempore of the Senate. It may happen that none of these individuals is able to serve. Then the office falls to the president's cabinet members. They would take office in the order in which each department was created:

Secretary of State

Secretary of the Treasury

Secretary of Defense

Attorney General

Secretary of the Interior

Secretary of Agriculture

Secretary of Commerce

Secretary of Labor

Secretary of Health and Human Services

Secretary of Housing and Urban Development

Secretary of Transportation

Secretary of Energy

Secretary of Education

Secretary of Veterans Affairs

Secretary of Homeland Security

Benefits

★ While in office, the president receives a salary. It is $400,000 per year. He or she lives in the White House. The president also has 24-hour Secret Service protection.

★ The president may travel on a Boeing 747 jet. This special jet is called Air Force One. It can hold 70 passengers. It has kitchens, a dining room, sleeping areas, and more. Air Force One can fly halfway around the world before needing to refuel. It can even refuel in flight!

★ When the president travels by car, he or she uses Cadillac One. It is a Cadillac Deville that has been modified. The car has heavy armor and communications systems. The president may even take Cadillac One along when visiting other countries.

★ The president also travels on a helicopter. It is called Marine One. It may also be taken along when the president visits other countries.

★ Sometimes the president needs to get away with family and friends. Camp David is the official presidential retreat. It is located in Maryland. The US Navy maintains the retreat. The US Marine Corps keeps it secure. The camp offers swimming, tennis, golf, and hiking.

★ When the president leaves office, he or she receives lifetime Secret Service protection. He or she also receives a yearly pension of $203,700. The former president also receives money for office space, supplies, and staff.

PRESIDENTS AND THEIR TERMS

PRESIDENT	PARTY	TOOK OFFICE	LEFT OFFICE	TERMS SERVED	VICE PRESIDENT
George Washington	None	April 30, 1789	March 4, 1797	Two	John Adams
John Adams	Federalist	March 4, 1797	March 4, 1801	One	Thomas Jefferson
Thomas Jefferson	Democratic-Republican	March 4, 1801	March 4, 1809	Two	Aaron Burr, George Clinton
James Madison	Democratic-Republican	March 4, 1809	March 4, 1817	Two	George Clinton, Elbridge Gerry
James Monroe	Democratic-Republican	March 4, 1817	March 4, 1825	Two	Daniel D. Tompkins
John Quincy Adams	Democratic-Republican	March 4, 1825	March 4, 1829	One	John C. Calhoun
Andrew Jackson	Democrat	March 4, 1829	March 4, 1837	Two	John C. Calhoun, Martin Van Buren
Martin Van Buren	Democrat	March 4, 1837	March 4, 1841	One	Richard M. Johnson
William H. Harrison	Whig	March 4, 1841	April 4, 1841	Died During First Term	John Tyler
John Tyler	Whig	April 6, 1841	March 4, 1845	Completed Harrison's Term	Office Vacant
James K. Polk	Democrat	March 4, 1845	March 4, 1849	One	George M. Dallas
Zachary Taylor	Whig	March 5, 1849	July 9, 1850	Died During First Term	Millard Fillmore

PRESIDENT	PARTY	TOOK OFFICE	LEFT OFFICE	TERMS SERVED	VICE PRESIDENT
Millard Fillmore	Whig	July 10, 1850	March 4, 1853	Completed Taylor's Term	Office Vacant
Franklin Pierce	Democrat	March 4, 1853	March 4, 1857	One	William R.D. King
James Buchanan	Democrat	March 4, 1857	March 4, 1861	One	John C. Breckinridge
Abraham Lincoln	Republican	March 4, 1861	April 15, 1865	Served One Term, Died During Second Term	Hannibal Hamlin, Andrew Johnson
Andrew Johnson	Democrat	April 15, 1865	March 4, 1869	Completed Lincoln's Second Term	Office Vacant
Ulysses S. Grant	Republican	March 4, 1869	March 4, 1877	Two	Schuyler Colfax, Henry Wilson
Rutherford B. Hayes	Republican	March 3, 1877	March 4, 1881	One	William A. Wheeler
James A. Garfield	Republican	March 4, 1881	September 19, 1881	Died During First Term	Chester Arthur
Chester Arthur	Republican	September 20, 1881	March 4, 1885	Completed Garfield's Term	Office Vacant
Grover Cleveland	Democrat	March 4, 1885	March 4, 1889	One	Thomas A. Hendricks
Benjamin Harrison	Republican	March 4, 1889	March 4, 1893	One	Levi P. Morton
Grover Cleveland	Democrat	March 4, 1893	March 4, 1897	One	Adlai E. Stevenson
William McKinley	Republican	March 4, 1897	September 14, 1901	Served One Term, Died During Second Term	Garret A. Hobart, Theodore Roosevelt

35

PRESIDENT	PARTY	TOOK OFFICE	LEFT OFFICE	TERMS SERVED	VICE PRESIDENT
Theodore Roosevelt	Republican	September 14, 1901	March 4, 1909	Completed McKinley's Second Term, Served One Term	Office Vacant, Charles Fairbanks
William Taft	Republican	March 4, 1909	March 4, 1913	One	James S. Sherman
Woodrow Wilson	Democrat	March 4, 1913	March 4, 1921	Two	Thomas R. Marshall
Warren G. Harding	Republican	March 4, 1921	August 2, 1923	Died During First Term	Calvin Coolidge
Calvin Coolidge	Republican	August 3, 1923	March 4, 1929	Completed Harding's Term, Served One Term	Office Vacant, Charles Dawes
Herbert Hoover	Republican	March 4, 1929	March 4, 1933	One	Charles Curtis
Franklin D. Roosevelt	Democrat	March 4, 1933	April 12, 1945	Served Three Terms, Died During Fourth Term	John Nance Garner, Henry A. Wallace, Harry S. Truman
Harry S. Truman	Democrat	April 12, 1945	January 20, 1953	Completed Roosevelt's Fourth Term, Served One Term	Office Vacant, Alben Barkley
Dwight D. Eisenhower	Republican	January 20, 1953	January 20, 1961	Two	Richard Nixon
John F. Kennedy	Democrat	January 20, 1961	November 22, 1963	Died During First Term	Lyndon B. Johnson
Lyndon B. Johnson	Democrat	November 22, 1963	January 20, 1969	Completed Kennedy's Term, Served One Term	Office Vacant, Hubert H. Humphrey
Richard Nixon	Republican	January 20, 1969	August 9, 1974	Completed First Term, Resigned During Second Term	Spiro T. Agnew, Gerald Ford

PRESIDENT	PARTY	TOOK OFFICE	LEFT OFFICE	TERMS SERVED	VICE PRESIDENT
Gerald Ford	Republican	August 9, 1974	January 20, 1977	Completed Nixon's Second Term	Nelson A. Rockefeller
Jimmy Carter	Democrat	January 20, 1977	January 20, 1981	One	Walter Mondale
Ronald Reagan	Republican	January 20, 1981	January 20, 1989	Two	George H.W. Bush
George H.W. Bush	Republican	January 20, 1989	January 20, 1993	One	Dan Quayle
Bill Clinton	Democrat	January 20, 1993	January 20, 2001	Two	Al Gore
George W. Bush	Republican	January 20, 2001	January 20, 2009	Two	Dick Cheney
Barack Obama	Democrat	January 20, 2009	January 20, 2017	Two	Joe Biden

"Freedom can never yield its fullness of blessings so long as the law or its administration places the smallest obstacle in the pathway of any virtuous citizen." James A. Garfield

★ WRITE TO THE PRESIDENT ★

You may write to the president at:
The White House
1600 Pennsylvania Avenue NW
Washington, DC 20500

You may e-mail the president at:
comments@whitehouse.gov

Glossary

American Civil War—the war between the Northern and Southern states from 1861 to 1865.

appoint—to choose someone to do a job.

assassin—someone who murders an important person by a surprise or secret attack.

civil service—the part of the government that is responsible for matters not covered by the military, the courts, or the law.

delegate—someone who represents other people at a meeting or in a lawmaking group.

graduation (gra-juh-WAY-shuhn)—an event held to mark the completion of a level of schooling.

investigate—to gather information about or study something.

lawyer (LAW-yuhr)—a person who gives people advice on laws or represents them in court.

nominate—to name as a possible winner.

politics—the art or science of government. Something referring to politics is political. A person who is active in politics is a politician.

Reconstruction—the period after the American Civil War when laws were passed to help the Southern states rebuild and return to the Union.

reform—to remove problems and make something better.

representative—someone chosen in an election to act or speak for the people who voted for him or her.

Republican—a member of the Republican political party.

reward—to give something as thanks for or recognition of someone's efforts.

scandal—an action that shocks people and disgraces those connected with it.

support—to believe in or be in favor of something.

trial—the hearing and judgment of a case in a courtroom or house of Congress.

★ WEBSITES ★

To learn more about the US Presidents, visit **booklinks.abdopublishing.com**. These links are routinely monitored and updated to provide the most current information available.

Index